Daily planner

This planner belongs to:

New day... new Goal

live your dream.

MEALS:
BREAKFAST

LUNCH

DINNER

PRIORITIES

APPOINTMENTS

TO DO

WATER
○ ○ ○ ○
○ ○ ○ ○

SELF CARE

THINGS TO BUY

GRATITUDE

NOTES

New day... new Goal

live your dream.

MEALS:

BREAKFAST

LUNCH

DINNER

PRIORITIES

APPOINTMENTS

TO DO

WATER
○ ○ ○ ○
○ ○ ○ ○

SELF CARE

GRATITUDE

THINGS TO BUY

NOTES

New day... new Goal

live your dream.

MEALS:
BREAKFAST

LUNCH

DINNER

PRIORITIES
_____
_____
_____
_____

APPOINTMENTS
_____
_____
_____
_____

TO DO
_____
_____
_____
_____
_____
_____
_____
_____
_____
_____
_____
_____

WATER
○ ○ ○ ○
○ ○ ○ ○

SELF CARE

GRATITUDE

THINGS TO BUY

NOTES

New day... new Goal

live your dream.

MEALS:
BREAKFAST

LUNCH

DINNER

PRIORITIES

APPOINTMENTS

TO DO

WATER
○ ○ ○ ○
○ ○ ○ ○

SELF CARE

THINGS TO BUY

GRATITUDE

NOTES

New day... new Goal

live your dream.

MEALS:
BREAKFAST

LUNCH

DINNER

PRIORITIES

APPOINTMENTS

TO DO

WATER
○ ○ ○ ○
○ ○ ○ ○

SELF CARE

THINGS TO BUY

GRATITUDE

NOTES

New day... new Goal

live your dream.

MEALS:
BREAKFAST

LUNCH

DINNER

PRIORITIES

APPOINTMENTS

TO DO

WATER
○ ○ ○ ○
○ ○ ○ ○

SELF CARE

THINGS TO BUY

GRATITUDE

NOTES

New day... new Goal

live your dream.

MEALS:

BREAKFAST

LUNCH

DINNER

PRIORITIES

APPOINTMENTS

TO DO

WATER
○ ○ ○ ○
○ ○ ○ ○

SELF CARE

THINGS TO BUY

GRATITUDE

NOTES

New day... new Goal

live your dream.

MEALS:
BREAKFAST

LUNCH

DINNER

PRIORITIES

APPOINTMENTS

TO DO

WATER
○ ○ ○ ○
○ ○ ○ ○

SELF CARE

THINGS TO BUY

GRATITUDE

NOTES

New day... new Goal

live your dream.

MEALS:

BREAKFAST

LUNCH

DINNER

PRIORITIES

APPOINTMENTS

TO DO

WATER
○ ○ ○ ○
○ ○ ○ ○

SELF CARE

THINGS TO BUY

GRATITUDE

NOTES

New day... new Goal

live your dream.

MEALS:
BREAKFAST

LUNCH

DINNER

GRATITUDE

NOTES

PRIORITIES

APPOINTMENTS

TO DO

WATER
○ ○ ○ ○
○ ○ ○ ○

SELF CARE

THINGS TO BUY

New day... new Goal

live your dream.

MEALS:
BREAKFAST

LUNCH

DINNER

PRIORITIES

APPOINTMENTS

TO DO

WATER
○ ○ ○ ○
○ ○ ○ ○

SELF CARE

GRATITUDE

THINGS TO BUY

NOTES

New day... new Goal

live your dream.

MEALS:
BREAKFAST

LUNCH

DINNER

PRIORITIES

APPOINTMENTS

TO DO

WATER
○ ○ ○ ○
○ ○ ○ ○

SELF CARE

THINGS TO BUY

GRATITUDE

NOTES

New day... new Goal

live your dream.

MEALS:

BREAKFAST

LUNCH

DINNER

PRIORITIES
_____
_____
_____
_____
_____

APPOINTMENTS
_____
_____
_____
_____

TO DO
_____
_____
_____
_____
_____
_____
_____
_____
_____
_____
_____
_____
_____
_____

WATER
○ ○ ○ ○
○ ○ ○ ○

SELF CARE

THINGS TO BUY

GRATITUDE

NOTES

New day... new Goal

live your dream.

MEALS:

BREAKFAST

LUNCH

DINNER

PRIORITIES

APPOINTMENTS

TO DO

WATER
○ ○ ○ ○
○ ○ ○ ○

SELF CARE

GRATITUDE

THINGS TO BUY

NOTES

New day... new Goal

live your dream.

MEALS:
BREAKFAST

LUNCH

DINNER

PRIORITIES

APPOINTMENTS

TO DO

WATER
○ ○ ○ ○
○ ○ ○ ○

SELF CARE

GRATITUDE

THINGS TO BUY

NOTES

New day... new Goal

live your dream.

MEALS:
BREAKFAST

LUNCH

DINNER

PRIORITIES
_____
_____
_____
_____

APPOINTMENTS
_____
_____
_____
_____

TO DO
_____
_____
_____
_____
_____
_____
_____
_____
_____
_____
_____
_____
_____
_____

WATER
○ ○ ○ ○
○ ○ ○ ○

SELF CARE

GRATITUDE

THINGS TO BUY

NOTES

New day... new Goal

live your dream.

MEALS:
BREAKFAST

LUNCH

DINNER

PRIORITIES

APPOINTMENTS

TO DO

WATER
○ ○ ○ ○
○ ○ ○ ○

SELF CARE

GRATITUDE

THINGS TO BUY

NOTES

New day... new Goal

live your dream.

MEALS:

BREAKFAST

LUNCH

DINNER

PRIORITIES

APPOINTMENTS

TO DO

WATER
○ ○ ○ ○
○ ○ ○ ○

SELF CARE

GRATITUDE

NOTES

THINGS TO BUY

New day... new Goal

live your dream.

MEALS:

BREAKFAST

LUNCH

DINNER

PRIORITIES

APPOINTMENTS

TO DO

WATER
○ ○ ○ ○
○ ○ ○ ○

SELF CARE

THINGS TO BUY

GRATITUDE

NOTES

New day... new Goal

live your dream.

MEALS:
BREAKFAST

LUNCH

DINNER

PRIORITIES
_____
_____
_____
_____
_____

APPOINTMENTS
_____
_____
_____
_____
_____

TO DO
_____
_____
_____
_____
_____
_____
_____
_____
_____
_____
_____
_____
_____
_____

WATER
○ ○ ○ ○
○ ○ ○ ○

SELF CARE

THINGS TO BUY

GRATITUDE

NOTES

New day... new Goal

live your dream.

MEALS:
BREAKFAST

LUNCH

DINNER

PRIORITIES

APPOINTMENTS

TO DO

WATER
○ ○ ○ ○
○ ○ ○ ○

SELF CARE

THINGS TO BUY

GRATITUDE

NOTES

New day... new Goal

live your dream.

MEALS:
BREAKFAST

LUNCH

DINNER

GRATITUDE

NOTES

PRIORITIES

APPOINTMENTS

TO DO

WATER
○ ○ ○ ○
○ ○ ○ ○

SELF CARE

THINGS TO BUY

New day... new Goal

live your dream.

MEALS:

BREAKFAST

LUNCH

DINNER

PRIORITIES

APPOINTMENTS

TO DO

WATER
○ ○ ○ ○
○ ○ ○ ○

SELF CARE

THINGS TO BUY

GRATITUDE

NOTES

New day... new Goal

live your dream.

MEALS:
BREAKFAST

LUNCH

DINNER

PRIORITIES

APPOINTMENTS

TO DO

WATER
○ ○ ○ ○
○ ○ ○ ○

SELF CARE

THINGS TO BUY

GRATITUDE

NOTES

New day... new Goal

live your dream.

MEALS:
BREAKFAST

LUNCH

DINNER

PRIORITIES

APPOINTMENTS

TO DO

WATER
○ ○ ○ ○
○ ○ ○ ○

SELF CARE

GRATITUDE

THINGS TO BUY

NOTES

New day... new Goal

live your dream.

MEALS:
BREAKFAST

LUNCH

DINNER

GRATITUDE

NOTES

PRIORITIES

APPOINTMENTS

TO DO

WATER
○ ○ ○ ○
○ ○ ○ ○

SELF CARE

THINGS TO BUY

New day... new Goal

live your dream.

MEALS:
BREAKFAST

LUNCH

DINNER

PRIORITIES
_____
_____
_____
_____
_____

APPOINTMENTS
_____
_____
_____
_____

TO DO
_____
_____
_____
_____
_____
_____
_____
_____
_____
_____
_____
_____
_____
_____

WATER
○ ○ ○ ○
○ ○ ○ ○

SELF CARE

GRATITUDE

NOTES

THINGS TO BUY

New day... new Goal

live your dream.

MEALS:
BREAKFAST

LUNCH

DINNER

GRATITUDE

NOTES

PRIORITIES

APPOINTMENTS

TO DO

WATER
○ ○ ○ ○
○ ○ ○ ○

SELF CARE

THINGS TO BUY

New day... new Goal

live your dream.

MEALS:
BREAKFAST

LUNCH

DINNER

PRIORITIES
_____
_____
_____
_____
_____

APPOINTMENTS
_____
_____
_____
_____
_____

TO DO
_____
_____
_____
_____
_____
_____
_____
_____
_____
_____
_____
_____
_____
_____

WATER
○ ○ ○ ○
○ ○ ○ ○

SELF CARE

THINGS TO BUY

GRATITUDE

NOTES

New day... new Goal

live your dream.

MEALS:

BREAKFAST

LUNCH

DINNER

PRIORITIES

APPOINTMENTS

TO DO

WATER

○ ○ ○ ○
○ ○ ○ ○

SELF CARE

THINGS TO BUY

GRATITUDE

NOTES

New day... new Goal

live your dream.

MEALS:
BREAKFAST

LUNCH

DINNER

PRIORITIES

APPOINTMENTS

TO DO

WATER
○ ○ ○ ○
○ ○ ○ ○

SELF CARE

THINGS TO BUY

GRATITUDE

NOTES

New day... new Goal

live your dream.

MEALS:
BREAKFAST

LUNCH

DINNER

PRIORITIES

APPOINTMENTS

TO DO

WATER
○ ○ ○ ○
○ ○ ○ ○

SELF CARE

THINGS TO BUY

GRATITUDE

NOTES

New day... new Goal

live your dream.

MEALS:
BREAKFAST

LUNCH

DINNER

PRIORITIES

APPOINTMENTS

TO DO

WATER
○ ○ ○ ○
○ ○ ○ ○

SELF CARE

GRATITUDE

THINGS TO BUY

NOTES

New day... new Goal

live your dream.

MEALS:

BREAKFAST

LUNCH

DINNER

PRIORITIES

APPOINTMENTS

TO DO

WATER
○ ○ ○ ○
○ ○ ○ ○

SELF CARE

THINGS TO BUY

GRATITUDE

NOTES

New day... new Goal

live your dream.

MEALS:

BREAKFAST

LUNCH

DINNER

PRIORITIES

APPOINTMENTS

TO DO

WATER
○ ○ ○ ○
○ ○ ○ ○

SELF CARE

THINGS TO BUY

GRATITUDE

NOTES

New day... new Goal

live your dream.

MEALS:

BREAKFAST

LUNCH

DINNER

PRIORITIES

APPOINTMENTS

TO DO

WATER
○ ○ ○ ○
○ ○ ○ ○

SELF CARE

GRATITUDE

THINGS TO BUY

NOTES

New day... new Goal

live your dream.

MEALS:

BREAKFAST

LUNCH

DINNER

PRIORITIES

APPOINTMENTS

TO DO

WATER
○ ○ ○ ○
○ ○ ○ ○

SELF CARE

GRATITUDE

NOTES

THINGS TO BUY

New day... new Goal

live your dream.

MEALS:
BREAKFAST

LUNCH

DINNER

PRIORITIES
_____
_____
_____
_____
_____

APPOINTMENTS
_____
_____
_____
_____
_____

TO DO
_____
_____
_____
_____
_____
_____
_____
_____
_____
_____
_____
_____
_____
_____
_____

WATER
○ ○ ○ ○
○ ○ ○ ○

SELF CARE

GRATITUDE

NOTES

THINGS TO BUY

New day... new Goal

live your dream.

MEALS:
BREAKFAST

LUNCH

DINNER

PRIORITIES

APPOINTMENTS

TO DO

WATER
○ ○ ○ ○
○ ○ ○ ○

SELF CARE

THINGS TO BUY

GRATITUDE

NOTES

New day... new Goal

live your dream.

MEALS:
BREAKFAST

LUNCH

DINNER

PRIORITIES

APPOINTMENTS

TO DO

WATER
○ ○ ○ ○
○ ○ ○ ○

SELF CARE

GRATITUDE

NOTES

THINGS TO BUY

New day... new Goal

live your dream.

MEALS:
BREAKFAST

LUNCH

DINNER

PRIORITIES

APPOINTMENTS

TO DO

WATER
○ ○ ○ ○
○ ○ ○ ○

SELF CARE

THINGS TO BUY

GRATITUDE

NOTES

New day... new Goal

live your dream.

MEALS:

BREAKFAST

LUNCH

DINNER

PRIORITIES

APPOINTMENTS

TO DO

WATER
○ ○ ○ ○
○ ○ ○ ○

SELF CARE

GRATITUDE

THINGS TO BUY

NOTES

New day... new Goal

live your dream.

MEALS:
BREAKFAST

LUNCH

DINNER

GRATITUDE

NOTES

PRIORITIES

APPOINTMENTS

TO DO

WATER
○ ○ ○ ○
○ ○ ○ ○

SELF CARE

THINGS TO BUY

New day... new Goal

live your dream.

MEALS:
BREAKFAST

LUNCH

DINNER

PRIORITIES

APPOINTMENTS

TO DO

WATER
○ ○ ○ ○
○ ○ ○ ○

SELF CARE

GRATITUDE

THINGS TO BUY

NOTES

New day... new Goal

live your dream.

MEALS:
BREAKFAST

LUNCH

DINNER

PRIORITIES
_____
_____
_____
_____

APPOINTMENTS
_____
_____
_____
_____

TO DO
_____
_____
_____
_____
_____
_____
_____
_____
_____
_____
_____
_____

WATER
○ ○ ○ ○
○ ○ ○ ○

SELF CARE

GRATITUDE

NOTES

THINGS TO BUY

New day... new Goal

live your dream.

MEALS:
BREAKFAST

LUNCH

DINNER

GRATITUDE

NOTES

PRIORITIES

APPOINTMENTS

TO DO

WATER
○ ○ ○ ○
○ ○ ○ ○

SELF CARE

THINGS TO BUY

New day... new Goal

live your dream.

MEALS:

BREAKFAST

LUNCH

DINNER

PRIORITIES

APPOINTMENTS

TO DO

WATER
○ ○ ○ ○
○ ○ ○ ○

SELF CARE

THINGS TO BUY

GRATITUDE

NOTES

New day... new Goal

live your dream.

MEALS:

BREAKFAST

LUNCH

DINNER

PRIORITIES

APPOINTMENTS

TO DO

WATER

○ ○ ○ ○
○ ○ ○ ○

SELF CARE

THINGS TO BUY

GRATITUDE

NOTES

New day... new Goal

live your dream.

MEALS:
BREAKFAST

LUNCH

DINNER

PRIORITIES

APPOINTMENTS

TO DO

WATER
○ ○ ○ ○
○ ○ ○ ○

SELF CARE

THINGS TO BUY

GRATITUDE

NOTES

New day... new Goal

live your dream.

MEALS:
BREAKFAST

LUNCH

DINNER

GRATITUDE

NOTES

PRIORITIES

APPOINTMENTS

TO DO

WATER
○ ○ ○ ○
○ ○ ○ ○

SELF CARE

THINGS TO BUY

New day... new Goal

live your dream.

MEALS:
BREAKFAST

LUNCH

DINNER

PRIORITIES

APPOINTMENTS

TO DO

WATER
○ ○ ○ ○
○ ○ ○ ○

SELF CARE

GRATITUDE

THINGS TO BUY

NOTES

New day... new Goal

live your dream.

MEALS:

BREAKFAST

LUNCH

DINNER

PRIORITIES

APPOINTMENTS

TO DO

WATER
○ ○ ○ ○
○ ○ ○ ○

SELF CARE

THINGS TO BUY

GRATITUDE

NOTES

New day... new Goal

live your dream.

MEALS:
BREAKFAST

LUNCH

DINNER

PRIORITIES

APPOINTMENTS

TO DO

WATER
○ ○ ○ ○
○ ○ ○ ○

SELF CARE

GRATITUDE

NOTES

THINGS TO BUY

New day... new Goal

live your dream.

MEALS:
BREAKFAST

LUNCH

DINNER

PRIORITIES
_____
_____
_____
_____
_____

APPOINTMENTS
_____
_____
_____
_____

TO DO
_____
_____
_____
_____
_____
_____
_____
_____
_____
_____
_____
_____

WATER
○ ○ ○ ○
○ ○ ○ ○

SELF CARE

THINGS TO BUY

GRATITUDE

NOTES

New day... new Goal

live your dream.

MEALS:
BREAKFAST

LUNCH

DINNER

PRIORITIES
_____
_____
_____
_____
_____

APPOINTMENTS
_____
_____
_____
_____

TO DO
_____
_____
_____
_____
_____
_____
_____
_____
_____
_____
_____
_____
_____

WATER
○ ○ ○ ○
○ ○ ○ ○

SELF CARE

GRATITUDE

THINGS TO BUY

NOTES

New day... new Goal

live your dream.

MEALS:

BREAKFAST

LUNCH

DINNER

PRIORITIES

APPOINTMENTS

TO DO

WATER
○ ○ ○ ○
○ ○ ○ ○

SELF CARE

GRATITUDE

THINGS TO BUY

NOTES

New day... new Goal

live your dream.

MEALS:
BREAKFAST

LUNCH

DINNER

PRIORITIES
_____
_____
_____
_____
_____

APPOINTMENTS
_____
_____
_____
_____
_____

TO DO
_____
_____
_____
_____
_____
_____
_____
_____
_____
_____
_____
_____
_____
_____

WATER
○ ○ ○ ○
○ ○ ○ ○

SELF CARE

THINGS TO BUY

GRATITUDE

NOTES

New day... new Goal

live your dream.

MEALS:
BREAKFAST

LUNCH

DINNER

PRIORITIES
_____
_____
_____
_____
_____

APPOINTMENTS
_____
_____
_____
_____

TO DO
_____
_____
_____
_____
_____
_____
_____
_____
_____
_____
_____
_____
_____

WATER
○ ○ ○ ○
○ ○ ○ ○

SELF CARE

GRATITUDE

THINGS TO BUY

NOTES

New day... new Goal

live your dream.

MEALS:
BREAKFAST

LUNCH

DINNER

GRATITUDE

NOTES

PRIORITIES

APPOINTMENTS

TO DO

WATER
○ ○ ○ ○
○ ○ ○ ○

SELF CARE

THINGS TO BUY

New day... new Goal

live your dream.

MEALS:

BREAKFAST

LUNCH

DINNER

PRIORITIES

APPOINTMENTS

TO DO

WATER
○ ○ ○ ○
○ ○ ○ ○

SELF CARE

THINGS TO BUY

GRATITUDE

NOTES

New day... new Goal

live your dream.

MEALS:
BREAKFAST

LUNCH

DINNER

PRIORITIES
_____
_____
_____
_____
_____

APPOINTMENTS
_____
_____
_____
_____
_____

TO DO
_____
_____
_____
_____
_____
_____
_____
_____
_____
_____
_____
_____
_____
_____

WATER
○ ○ ○ ○
○ ○ ○ ○

SELF CARE

GRATITUDE

NOTES

THINGS TO BUY

New day... new Goal

live your dream.

MEALS:

BREAKFAST

LUNCH

DINNER

GRATITUDE

NOTES

PRIORITIES

APPOINTMENTS

TO DO

WATER

○ ○ ○ ○
○ ○ ○ ○

SELF CARE

THINGS TO BUY

New day... new Goal

live your dream.

MEALS:

BREAKFAST

LUNCH

DINNER

PRIORITIES
_____
_____
_____
_____

APPOINTMENTS
_____
_____
_____
_____

TO DO
_____
_____
_____
_____
_____
_____
_____
_____
_____
_____
_____
_____
_____

WATER
○ ○ ○ ○
○ ○ ○ ○

SELF CARE

GRATITUDE

NOTES

THINGS TO BUY

New day... new Goal

live your dream.

MEALS:
BREAKFAST

LUNCH

DINNER

PRIORITIES

APPOINTMENTS

TO DO

WATER
○ ○ ○ ○
○ ○ ○ ○

SELF CARE

THINGS TO BUY

GRATITUDE

NOTES

New day... new Goal

live your dream.

MEALS:
BREAKFAST

LUNCH

DINNER

PRIORITIES

APPOINTMENTS

TO DO

WATER
○ ○ ○ ○
○ ○ ○ ○

SELF CARE

THINGS TO BUY

GRATITUDE

NOTES

New day... new Goal

live your dream.

MEALS:
BREAKFAST

LUNCH

DINNER

PRIORITIES

APPOINTMENTS

TO DO

WATER
○ ○ ○ ○
○ ○ ○ ○

SELF CARE

GRATITUDE

NOTES

THINGS TO BUY

New day... new Goal

live your dream.

MEALS:

BREAKFAST

LUNCH

DINNER

PRIORITIES

APPOINTMENTS

TO DO

WATER
○ ○ ○ ○
○ ○ ○ ○

SELF CARE

THINGS TO BUY

GRATITUDE

NOTES

New day... new Goal

live your dream.

MEALS:

BREAKFAST

LUNCH

DINNER

PRIORITIES

APPOINTMENTS

TO DO

WATER
○ ○ ○ ○
○ ○ ○ ○

SELF CARE

GRATITUDE

NOTES

THINGS TO BUY

New day... new Goal

live your dream.

MEALS:
BREAKFAST

LUNCH

DINNER

PRIORITIES

APPOINTMENTS

TO DO

WATER
○ ○ ○ ○
○ ○ ○ ○

SELF CARE

GRATITUDE

NOTES

THINGS TO BUY

New day... new Goal

live your dream.

MEALS:

BREAKFAST

LUNCH

DINNER

PRIORITIES

APPOINTMENTS

TO DO

WATER
○ ○ ○ ○
○ ○ ○ ○

SELF CARE

GRATITUDE

NOTES

THINGS TO BUY

New day... new Goal

live your dream.

MEALS:
BREAKFAST

LUNCH

DINNER

PRIORITIES

APPOINTMENTS

TO DO

WATER
○ ○ ○ ○
○ ○ ○ ○

SELF CARE

THINGS TO BUY

GRATITUDE

NOTES

New day... new Goal

live your dream.

MEALS:

BREAKFAST

LUNCH

DINNER

PRIORITIES

APPOINTMENTS

TO DO

WATER
◯ ◯ ◯ ◯
◯ ◯ ◯ ◯

SELF CARE

GRATITUDE

THINGS TO BUY

NOTES

New day... new Goal

live your dream.

MEALS:
BREAKFAST

LUNCH

DINNER

GRATITUDE

NOTES

PRIORITIES

APPOINTMENTS

TO DO

WATER
○ ○ ○ ○
○ ○ ○ ○

SELF CARE

THINGS TO BUY

New day... new Goal

live your dream.

MEALS:

BREAKFAST

LUNCH

DINNER

PRIORITIES

APPOINTMENTS

TO DO

WATER
○ ○ ○ ○
○ ○ ○ ○

SELF CARE

GRATITUDE

NOTES

THINGS TO BUY

New day... new Goal

live your dream.

MEALS:
BREAKFAST

LUNCH

DINNER

PRIORITIES

APPOINTMENTS

TO DO

WATER
○ ○ ○ ○
○ ○ ○ ○

SELF CARE

THINGS TO BUY

GRATITUDE

NOTES

New day... new Goal

live your dream.

MEALS:
BREAKFAST

LUNCH

DINNER

GRATITUDE

NOTES

PRIORITIES

APPOINTMENTS

TO DO

WATER
○ ○ ○ ○
○ ○ ○ ○

SELF CARE

THINGS TO BUY

New day... new Goal

live your dream.

MEALS:

BREAKFAST

LUNCH

DINNER

PRIORITIES

APPOINTMENTS

TO DO

WATER
○ ○ ○ ○
○ ○ ○ ○

SELF CARE

THINGS TO BUY

GRATITUDE

NOTES

New day... new Goal

live your dream.

MEALS:
BREAKFAST

LUNCH

DINNER

PRIORITIES

APPOINTMENTS

TO DO

WATER
○ ○ ○ ○
○ ○ ○ ○

SELF CARE

THINGS TO BUY

GRATITUDE

NOTES

New day... new Goal

live your dream.

MEALS:
BREAKFAST

LUNCH

DINNER

PRIORITIES

APPOINTMENTS

TO DO

WATER
○ ○ ○ ○
○ ○ ○ ○

SELF CARE

THINGS TO BUY

GRATITUDE

NOTES

New day... new Goal

live your dream.

MEALS:
BREAKFAST

LUNCH

DINNER

PRIORITIES

APPOINTMENTS

TO DO

WATER
○ ○ ○ ○
○ ○ ○ ○

SELF CARE

GRATITUDE

NOTES

THINGS TO BUY

New day... new Goal

live your dream.

MEALS:

BREAKFAST

LUNCH

DINNER

PRIORITIES

APPOINTMENTS

TO DO

WATER
○ ○ ○ ○
○ ○ ○ ○

SELF CARE

THINGS TO BUY

GRATITUDE

NOTES

New day... new Goal

live your dream.

MEALS:
BREAKFAST

LUNCH

DINNER

PRIORITIES

APPOINTMENTS

TO DO

WATER
○ ○ ○ ○
○ ○ ○ ○

SELF CARE

THINGS TO BUY

GRATITUDE

NOTES

New day... new Goal

live your dream.

MEALS:
BREAKFAST

LUNCH

DINNER

GRATITUDE

NOTES

PRIORITIES

APPOINTMENTS

TO DO

WATER
○ ○ ○ ○
○ ○ ○ ○

SELF CARE

THINGS TO BUY

New day... new Goal

live your dream.

MEALS:
BREAKFAST

LUNCH

DINNER

PRIORITIES
_____
_____
_____
_____

APPOINTMENTS
_____
_____
_____
_____

TO DO
_____
_____
_____
_____
_____
_____
_____
_____
_____
_____
_____
_____
_____

WATER
○ ○ ○ ○
○ ○ ○ ○

SELF CARE

GRATITUDE

THINGS TO BUY

NOTES

New day... new Goal

live your dream.

MEALS:
BREAKFAST

LUNCH

DINNER

PRIORITIES

APPOINTMENTS

TO DO

WATER
○ ○ ○ ○
○ ○ ○ ○

SELF CARE

GRATITUDE

THINGS TO BUY

NOTES

New day... new Goal

live your dream.

MEALS:

BREAKFAST

LUNCH

DINNER

PRIORITIES

APPOINTMENTS

TO DO

WATER
○ ○ ○ ○
○ ○ ○ ○

SELF CARE

GRATITUDE

NOTES

THINGS TO BUY

New day... new Goal

live your dream.

MEALS:
BREAKFAST

LUNCH

DINNER

PRIORITIES

APPOINTMENTS

TO DO

WATER
○ ○ ○ ○
○ ○ ○ ○

SELF CARE

THINGS TO BUY

GRATITUDE

NOTES

New day... new Goal

live your dream.

MEALS:
BREAKFAST

LUNCH

DINNER

PRIORITIES

APPOINTMENTS

TO DO

WATER
○ ○ ○ ○
○ ○ ○ ○

SELF CARE

GRATITUDE

NOTES

THINGS TO BUY

New day... new Goal

live your dream.

MEALS:
BREAKFAST

LUNCH

DINNER

PRIORITIES

APPOINTMENTS

TO DO

WATER
○ ○ ○ ○
○ ○ ○ ○

SELF CARE

THINGS TO BUY

GRATITUDE

NOTES

New day... new Goal

live your dream.

MEALS:

BREAKFAST

LUNCH

DINNER

PRIORITIES

APPOINTMENTS

TO DO

WATER
○ ○ ○ ○
○ ○ ○ ○

SELF CARE

GRATITUDE

NOTES

THINGS TO BUY

New day... new Goal

live your dream.

MEALS:
BREAKFAST

LUNCH

DINNER

PRIORITIES

APPOINTMENTS

TO DO

WATER
○ ○ ○ ○
○ ○ ○ ○

SELF CARE

GRATITUDE

THINGS TO BUY

NOTES

New day... new Goal

live your dream.

MEALS:

BREAKFAST

LUNCH

DINNER

PRIORITIES

_____
_____
_____
_____

APPOINTMENTS

_____
_____
_____
_____

TO DO

_____
_____
_____
_____
_____
_____
_____
_____
_____
_____
_____
_____

WATER

○ ○ ○ ○
○ ○ ○ ○

SELF CARE

THINGS TO BUY

GRATITUDE

NOTES

New day... new Goal

live your dream.

MEALS:
BREAKFAST

LUNCH

DINNER

PRIORITIES

APPOINTMENTS

TO DO

WATER
○ ○ ○ ○
○ ○ ○ ○

SELF CARE

THINGS TO BUY

GRATITUDE

NOTES

New day... new Goal

live your dream.

MEALS:

BREAKFAST

LUNCH

DINNER

PRIORITIES

APPOINTMENTS

TO DO

WATER
○ ○ ○ ○
○ ○ ○ ○

SELF CARE

GRATITUDE

THINGS TO BUY

NOTES

New day... new Goal

live your dream.

MEALS:
BREAKFAST

LUNCH

DINNER

PRIORITIES

APPOINTMENTS

TO DO

WATER
○ ○ ○ ○
○ ○ ○ ○

SELF CARE

THINGS TO BUY

GRATITUDE

NOTES

New day... new Goal

live your dream.

MEALS:
BREAKFAST

LUNCH

DINNER

PRIORITIES

APPOINTMENTS

TO DO

WATER
○ ○ ○ ○
○ ○ ○ ○

SELF CARE

GRATITUDE

NOTES

THINGS TO BUY

New day... new Goal

live your dream.

MEALS:

BREAKFAST

LUNCH

DINNER

PRIORITIES

APPOINTMENTS

TO DO

WATER
○ ○ ○ ○
○ ○ ○ ○

SELF CARE

THINGS TO BUY

GRATITUDE

NOTES

New day... new Goal

live your dream.

MEALS:
BREAKFAST

LUNCH

DINNER

GRATITUDE

NOTES

PRIORITIES

APPOINTMENTS

TO DO

WATER
○ ○ ○ ○
○ ○ ○ ○

SELF CARE

THINGS TO BUY

New day... new Goal

live your dream.

MEALS:
BREAKFAST

LUNCH

DINNER

PRIORITIES

APPOINTMENTS

TO DO

WATER
○ ○ ○ ○
○ ○ ○ ○

SELF CARE

THINGS TO BUY

GRATITUDE

NOTES

New day... new Goal

live your dream.

MEALS:
BREAKFAST

LUNCH

DINNER

PRIORITIES
_____
_____
_____
_____
_____

APPOINTMENTS
_____
_____
_____
_____

TO DO
_____
_____
_____
_____
_____
_____
_____
_____
_____
_____
_____
_____
_____

WATER
○ ○ ○ ○
○ ○ ○ ○

SELF CARE

GRATITUDE

THINGS TO BUY

NOTES

New day... new Goal

live your dream.

MEALS:
BREAKFAST

LUNCH

DINNER

PRIORITIES

APPOINTMENTS

TO DO

WATER
○ ○ ○ ○
○ ○ ○ ○

SELF CARE

GRATITUDE

THINGS TO BUY

NOTES

New day... new Goal

live your dream.

MEALS:

BREAKFAST

LUNCH

DINNER

PRIORITIES

APPOINTMENTS

TO DO

WATER
○ ○ ○ ○
○ ○ ○ ○

SELF CARE

GRATITUDE

THINGS TO BUY

NOTES

New day... new Goal

live your dream.

MEALS:
BREAKFAST

LUNCH

DINNER

PRIORITIES

APPOINTMENTS

TO DO

WATER
○ ○ ○ ○
○ ○ ○ ○

SELF CARE

GRATITUDE

THINGS TO BUY

NOTES

New day... new Goal

live your dream.

MEALS:
BREAKFAST

LUNCH

DINNER

GRATITUDE

NOTES

PRIORITIES

APPOINTMENTS

TO DO

WATER
○ ○ ○ ○
○ ○ ○ ○

SELF CARE

THINGS TO BUY

New day... new Goal

live your dream.

MEALS:
BREAKFAST

LUNCH

DINNER

PRIORITIES

APPOINTMENTS

TO DO

WATER
○ ○ ○ ○
○ ○ ○ ○

SELF CARE

GRATITUDE

THINGS TO BUY

NOTES

New day... new Goal

live your dream.

MEALS:

BREAKFAST

LUNCH

DINNER

PRIORITIES

APPOINTMENTS

TO DO

WATER
○ ○ ○ ○
○ ○ ○ ○

SELF CARE

GRATITUDE

NOTES

THINGS TO BUY

New day... new Goal

live your dream.

MEALS:
BREAKFAST

LUNCH

DINNER

PRIORITIES
_____
_____
_____
_____
_____

APPOINTMENTS
_____
_____
_____
_____
_____

TO DO
_____
_____
_____
_____
_____
_____
_____
_____
_____
_____
_____
_____
_____
_____

WATER
◯ ◯ ◯ ◯
◯ ◯ ◯ ◯

SELF CARE

THINGS TO BUY

GRATITUDE

NOTES

New day... new Goal

live your dream.

MEALS:
BREAKFAST

LUNCH

DINNER

PRIORITIES

APPOINTMENTS

TO DO

WATER
○ ○ ○ ○
○ ○ ○ ○

SELF CARE

GRATITUDE

NOTES

THINGS TO BUY

New day... new Goal

live your dream.

MEALS:
BREAKFAST

LUNCH

DINNER

PRIORITIES
_____
_____
_____
_____
_____

APPOINTMENTS
_____
_____
_____
_____
_____

TO DO
_____
_____
_____
_____
_____
_____
_____
_____
_____
_____
_____
_____
_____
_____

WATER
○ ○ ○ ○
○ ○ ○ ○

SELF CARE

GRATITUDE

NOTES

THINGS TO BUY

New day... new Goal

live your dream.

MEALS:
BREAKFAST

LUNCH

DINNER

GRATITUDE

NOTES

PRIORITIES

APPOINTMENTS

TO DO

WATER
○ ○ ○ ○
○ ○ ○ ○

SELF CARE

THINGS TO BUY

New day... new Goal

live your dream.

MEALS:

BREAKFAST

LUNCH

DINNER

PRIORITIES

APPOINTMENTS

TO DO

WATER
○ ○ ○ ○
○ ○ ○ ○

SELF CARE

THINGS TO BUY

GRATITUDE

NOTES

New day... new Goal

live your dream.

MEALS:

BREAKFAST

LUNCH

DINNER

PRIORITIES

APPOINTMENTS

TO DO

WATER
○ ○ ○ ○
○ ○ ○ ○

SELF CARE

THINGS TO BUY

GRATITUDE

NOTES

New day... new Goal

live your dream.

MEALS:
BREAKFAST

LUNCH

DINNER

PRIORITIES
_____
_____
_____
_____
_____

APPOINTMENTS
_____
_____
_____
_____
_____

TO DO
_____
_____
_____
_____
_____
_____
_____
_____
_____
_____
_____
_____
_____

WATER
○ ○ ○ ○
○ ○ ○ ○

SELF CARE

GRATITUDE

THINGS TO BUY

NOTES

New day... new Goal

live your dream.

MEALS:

BREAKFAST

LUNCH

DINNER

PRIORITIES

APPOINTMENTS

TO DO

WATER
○ ○ ○ ○
○ ○ ○ ○

SELF CARE

GRATITUDE

THINGS TO BUY

NOTES

New day... new Goal

live your dream.

MEALS:
BREAKFAST

LUNCH

DINNER

PRIORITIES

APPOINTMENTS

TO DO

WATER
○ ○ ○ ○
○ ○ ○ ○

SELF CARE

GRATITUDE

NOTES

THINGS TO BUY

New day... new Goal

live your dream.

MEALS:
BREAKFAST

LUNCH

DINNER

PRIORITIES

APPOINTMENTS

TO DO

WATER
○ ○ ○ ○
○ ○ ○ ○

SELF CARE

THINGS TO BUY

GRATITUDE

NOTES

Printed by Libri Plureos GmbH in Hamburg, Germany